EDGE BOOKS™

TRUE TALES OF
SURVIVAL
PRESENTS:

SHIPWRECK!

DEBBIE KILEY'S STORY OF SURVIVAL

by Tim O'Shei

Consultant:
Al Siebert, PhD
Author of *The Survivor Personality*

Capstone
press®

Mankato, Minnesota

Edge Books are published by Capstone Press,
151 Good Counsel Drive, P.O. Box 669, Mankato, Minnesota 56002.
www.capstonepress.com

Library of Congress Cataloging-in-Publication Data
O'Shei, Tim.
    Shipwreck!: Debbie Kiley's story of survival / by Tim O'Shei.
    p. cm.—(Edge Books. True tales of survival)
    Summary: "Describes how sailor Debbie Kiley survived a shipwreck and several
days adrift in the Atlantic Ocean"—Provided by publisher.
    Includes bibliographical references and index.
    ISBN-13: 978-1-4296-0089-7 (hardcover)
    ISBN-10: 1-4296-0089-6 (hardcover)
    1. Trashman (Yacht)—Juvenile literature. 2. Shipwrecks—North Atlantic Ocean—
Juvenile literature. 3. Kiley, Deborah Scaling—Juvenile literature. 4. Survival after
airplane accidents, shipwrecks, etc.—Juvenile literature. I. Title. II. Series.
G530.T727O84 2008
910.9163'48—dc22   2006102272

Editorial Credits
Angie Kaelberer, editor; Jason Knudson, set designer; Kyle Grenz, book designer;
    Charlene Deyle and Scott Thoms, photo researchers

Photo Credits
BigStockPhoto.com/buso23, 4–5
Corbis/Neil Rabinowitz, 27 (foreground); Royalty-Free, 22–23; Tony Arruza, 14–15
Getty Images Inc./Frederick M. Brown, 29 (foreground)
The Image Works/Bob Daemmrich, 12–13
James P. Rowan, 11 (foreground)
SAFMC/K. Iverson, 18–19
Shutterstock/Andriy Rovenko, cover, 32; Bridget Zawitoski, 20–21; Dan Collier,
    26–27 (background); jarvis gray, 1; Kevin Norris, 10–11 (background);
    Mark Bond, 2–3; pls, 24–25; Pling, 30–31; Sjanie Gonlag, 16–17; Taiga, 8–9;
    trialart-info, 28–29
SuperStock, Inc./Andrew Dawson, 6–7

1 2 3 4 5 6 12 11 10 09 08 07

TABLE OF CONTENTS

CHAPTER 1

SWIMMING WITH SHARKS

LEARN ABOUT:

- Something lurks below
- Sharks!
- A test of courage

All Debbie and her friends could see
was endless miles of ocean.

"Don't kick me!" Mark Adams yelled.

Debbie was confused. She hadn't kicked Mark. She was floating in the middle of the Atlantic Ocean. One day earlier, the yacht she was sailing had sunk, leaving Debbie and her four crewmates clinging to the side of an inflatable boat.

Now, three of Debbie's companions were sitting safely inside the boat. Debbie and Mark were in the water, which was much warmer than the cold, windy air.

Debbie didn't understand why Mark thought she was kicking him. "I'm not touching you," she said.

But Mark insisted that she was kicking him. Debbie knew she wasn't. She ducked her head underwater to see what was brushing against Mark's legs. What she saw made her heart thump like a bass drum.

Sharks! Dozens of sharks! Some were close enough to chomp off her legs.

Debbie burst to the surface and yelled. She and Mark scrambled into the boat.

Five people were alone at sea. They had no food or drinking water. Fearsome predators surrounded their inflatable boat. The ocean was testing their strength and courage. Only some of them would survive.

Sharks! Dozens of sharks!

Razor-toothed sharks circled underneath the inflatable boat.

CHAPTER 2

A BORN SAILOR

Debbie worked as a crewmember on yachts.

8

LEARN ABOUT:

- **Love of boats**
- **Suspicious signs**
- **Storms at sea**

Debbie Kiley was born Debbie Scaling in 1958. Her childhood was unhappy. Her parents divorced when she was a baby. Her mother went on to have four more marriages. During one of those relationships, Debbie was abused. She developed an eating disorder called bulimia, which she still struggled with as an adult.

Debbie learned to sail when she was 8 years old at a summer camp. As she grew older, she found that she loved the water and being outdoors. She was happiest when she was sailing or working on a boat.

A CAREER IN SAILING

After high school, Debbie enrolled at the University of Texas but left after three years. She devoted herself to sailing and enjoyed success as a member of racing crews. She was the first American woman to finish a famous competition called the Whitbread Round the World Race.

Whenever one crew job ended, Debbie began looking for the next. That was the case in the fall of 1982. Debbie was in Bar Harbor, Maine, but wanted to head south to get another racing job. She met John Lippoth, who had been hired as the captain of a 58-foot (18-meter) yacht called *Trashman.* John was delivering the yacht to Fort Lauderdale, Florida, and needed crewmembers. Debbie liked the idea of getting paid to travel to warm and sunny Florida. She took the job.

SHAKY SIGNS

As Debbie worked with John to prepare the boat for voyage, she became uneasy. The ship was cluttered. The sails needed to be tighter. The engine wasn't running well. When Debbie talked to other experienced sailors, they told her that John didn't have a good reputation.

The situation didn't improve as the other crewmembers joined them. John brought his girlfriend, Meg Mooney, even though she wasn't a sailor.

Later, in Annapolis, Maryland, John hired Brad Cavanagh and Mark Adams. Brad was the younger brother of Debbie's friend Sarah, and she trusted him. But Mark was loud and liked to argue. That only added to Debbie's nerves. She considered quitting, but John told her if she did, he would make sure she never got another job on a boat.

Debbie stayed, but a bad feeling lurked in her gut.

In the fall of 1982, Debbie was looking for a job in Bar Harbor, Maine.

SAILING INTO DANGER

Trashman left Annapolis in the third week of October. Within a couple of days, the weather at sea turned bad. The crew didn't realize it, but a hurricane had hit. The winds whipped up the sea like a milkshake. The waves were 35 to 45 feet (11 to 14 meters) high. The wind gusted to 100 miles (161 kilometers) per hour.

While the weather battered the boat, Debbie and Brad stood watch for 11 hours. Meanwhile, John tried to get the ship's generator running in case they lost power. Mark had been drinking and was no help. Meg came up on deck to try to help, but she fell as the boat rocked, hurting her back.

John called the Coast Guard and asked for help. The Coast Guard radioed back that two merchant ships were in the area and would come to help *Trashman*'s crew. But it would take the ships at least five hours to get there.

We've got to go now!

Soon after setting sail, the crew ran into a huge storm.

With John and Mark standing watch, Debbie tried to get some rest. It didn't last. Brad woke her and screamed, "We've got to go now!" Water had crashed through the windows and flooded the boat. *Trashman* was sinking.

13

CHAPTER 3

SURVIVAL AT SEA

LEARN ABOUT:

- Trashman sinks
- Trapped in a raft
- Focusing on survival

Trashman couldn't withstand the massive storm.

The crewmembers sloshed through the shoulder-deep water in the cabin and scrambled on deck. Mark untied the life raft, but the wind swept it away. Brad untied the 12-foot (4-meter) Zodiac inflatable boat, which the crew usually used to travel from the yacht to the shore. He held on to the boat in the water as the rest of the crew jumped into the ocean.

After a long struggle, the crewmembers managed to grab hold of the upside-down Zodiac. The crewmembers stayed underneath, where the boat formed a protective shell from the weather. Each of them was cut and bruised. Meg's injuries were the worst. Her deep cuts were almost to the bone.

As the five clung to the Zodiac, they watched *Trashman* sink into the sea. It was 2:00 in the afternoon of October 24. The crew was stranded in the Atlantic Ocean. There was no food, no rescuers, and no land. Debbie had never been more afraid in her life.

STRUGGLING TO STAY WARM

The water was 76 degrees Fahrenheit (24 degrees Celsius). It was much warmer than the 40-degree Fahrenheit (4-degree Celsius) air. For the next 18 hours, the *Trashman* crew treaded water. The sailors were cold and tired. They figured out a way to share body heat and get rest. Brad and John grabbed a rope line. They put their legs on a wire that stretched across the boat and laid their heads on the inside of a rubber cover. Only their backs touched the water. Debbie and Mark then rested on top of Brad and John.

Meg was badly injured and needed warmth and rest the most. But she was afraid of enclosed spaces and wouldn't join the group huddled under the boat. Instead, she clung to the outside of the Zodiac.

EDGE FACT

Trashman sank in the Gulf Stream. This stretch of warm water begins in the Caribbean Sea. It flows through the Gulf of Mexico and along the eastern U.S. coast.

The weather improved by the next morning. The crew turned over the Zodiac. John, Meg, and Brad got in first. Debbie and Mark were still in the water. That's when Mark told Debbie to stop kicking him. Debbie dunked her head under the water and saw dozens of sharks circling below. She popped to the surface and yelled "Sharks!"

Nothing more needed to be said. Debbie and Mark scrambled into the safety of the Zodiac.

17

Sharks threatened the crew's safety.

ADRIFT AT SEA

By the third day, the bad situation had turned worse. Meg's wounds were puffy and oozing pus. Red streaks stretched from her legs to her upper body. She had blood poisoning. Debbie realized Meg was going to die.

The rest of the crew was in grave danger too. Their cuts were getting infected. Without water to drink, they were dehydrated. The cold air put them at risk for hypothermia.

Floating seaweed helped keep the crew warm.

Several times, they saw a ship pass by in the distance. They waved and yelled, trying to get someone's attention, but had no luck. They had long given up hope that the Coast Guard was coming to the rescue. *Trashman*'s crew was clearly alone.

A MENTAL CHALLENGE

The crew was cold, thirsty, and cramped. But their biggest challenge was mental. They had to concentrate on surviving.

Though Debbie was scared, she made good decisions. When the boat floated through a bed of seaweed, she convinced her crewmates to gather it and use it to cover themselves like a blanket.

Debbie struggled to fight off her fears. She focused on simple things to keep herself calm. Sometimes she stared at the sky and thought about the clouds. Other times, she gazed at the many small creatures that lived in the seaweed. Debbie also thought about her mother. She hoped to see her mom again and perhaps build a better relationship with her.

Brad found a focus too. He gave himself the job of keeping the boat balanced. Brad and Debbie also made an agreement to take care of each other. They tried to take turns sleeping. While one was asleep, the other's job was to keep watch on the safety of the boat.

EDGE FACT

The Coast Guard received an incorrect report that *Trashman* had made it safely to Wilmington, North Carolina. They never found out who made this call.

Meanwhile, John and Mark were falling apart. Mark had been fighting, especially with Debbie, the whole time. On the evening of the third day at sea, John and Mark leaned over the side of the Zodiac. They gulped down mouthfuls of seawater. Debbie knew that was a terrible mistake.

21

Ocean water isn't safe for people to drink.

CHAPTER 4

A MIRACLE RESCUE

LEARN ABOUT:
- Crew overboard
- Rescue by Russians
- Return to the sea

Shark attacks killed two of Debbie's crewmates.

Mark and John's thirst led them to drink from the ocean. But drinking saltwater is one of the worst things a person can do. An overload of salt in the body causes the kidneys to stop working. It also damages the nervous system and the brain. That most likely explains what happened to Mark and John on the fourth day at sea. They began talking about cigarettes and sandwiches they had brought with them. Then they started searching around the Zodiac for them. Of course, there were none.

SHARK ATTACKS

Then John told his crewmates that he saw land. They were at least 100 miles (161 kilometers) from the shore. But John insisted he saw land and jumped overboard. He swam a short distance. A gut-wrenching scream ripped through the air. John's head disappeared below the water. A shark had killed him.

A few hours later, Mark said he was going to the 7-Eleven store. He jumped overboard. The Zodiac started shaking from below. The water turned bubbly and red.

23

The sharks had eaten Mark right under the boat. Long after they were done with his body, they kept circling and ramming themselves against the Zodiac. It was as if the sharks knew that Debbie, Brad, and Meg were in there. The threesome lay still for hours, frozen in fear. Finally, the sharks left.

DEATH AT SEA

Meg died during the fourth night. The next morning, Debbie and Brad removed her jewelry to give to her family. They gently floated her body into the water. They then said a prayer and turned away. They were the only two left.

A Russian freighter rescued Debbie and Brad.

The bottom of the boat was filled with water dirtied by urine, rotting seaweed, and pus. The smell was unbearable.

Debbie and Brad got out of the boat, turned it upside down, and splashed water to wash it out. After they flipped it back, Debbie pulled herself back inside. But Brad struggled. He was too weak to make the climb easily. Debbie was worried that the sharks would return. After a half-hour, she was finally able to help Brad back into the boat.

The pair turned their focus to catching some fish. They hadn't eaten since *Trashman* sank. Their attention switched, though, when they saw a ship in the distance. Debbie wasn't excited, because other ships had sailed by without seeing them. But this time, somebody on the ship spotted them! The ship came closer and closer as Debbie and Brad screamed and waved from the boat.

RESCUE!

When the ship was about 150 feet (46 meters) from the Zodiac, a crewmember threw a rope with a floating ring into the ocean. Debbie and Brad jumped off the Zodiac and swam. Brad slipped his body through the ring and grabbed onto Debbie, who was clinging to the rope. The sailors on the ship began hauling them in.

As Debbie and Brad neared the freighter, they were pulled underwater. They scraped the side of the ship. As the sailors pulled the rope upward, Debbie and Brad dangled from the rope. Again, they slammed into the side of the ship.

Finally, Debbie and Brad were lifted to safety. The ship turned out to be a Russian freighter on its way to Canada. The ship operators got in touch with a U.S. Coast Guard boat, which came and picked up Debbie and Brad.

The Coast Guard crew took Brad and Debbie to North Carolina, where they spent eight days in a hospital. They were treated for dehydration and infections.

A Coast Guard rescue boat helped Debbie and Brad.

EDGE FACT

Debbie's story has been featured on several TV shows and was made into a TV movie called *Two Came Back*.

FEAR OF THE WATER

While Brad began sailing again shortly after the rescue, Debbie didn't. She struggled with the *Trashman* experience for years. She had nightmares and wanted to avoid the water.

In 1984, Debbie married yacht designer John Kiley, who helped her start sailing again. Debbie and John had two children, Marka and Quatro, but later divorced. In 1994, Debbie wrote a book called *Albatross* about the sinking. She said writing the book helped her deal with the bad memories. In 2006, she published another book, *No Victims Only Survivors*.

A NEW LIFE

Today, Debbie lives in Texas with her second husband, Greg Blackmon. She works in the fitness business and gives speeches about her experience to both students and adults.

Debbie talks to her audiences about the keys to survival. One of them is to believe you will live. During the five days that followed the sinking, Debbie experienced fear, anger, and sadness. But she never believed she would die. Her attitude and mental toughness helped her survive.

Today, Debbie speaks to others about her survival story.

GLOSSARY

bulimia (buh-LEE-mee-uh)—an eating disorder in which a person overeats and then purposely vomits the food

dehydration (dee-hye-DRAY-shuhn)—a life-threatening medical condition caused by a lack of water

freighter (FRAY-tur)—a ship that carries goods

generator (JEN-uh-ray-tur)—a machine that produces electricity by turning a magnet inside a coil of wire

hypothermia (hye-puh-THUR-mee-uh)—a life-threatening medical condition resulting from a drop in body temperature

pus (PUHS)—a yellowish-white fluid found in sores and infections

30

yacht (YAHT)—a large boat used for sailing or racing

READ MORE

O'Shei, Tim. *The World's Most Amazing Survival Stories.* The World's Top Tens. Mankato, Minn.: Capstone Press, 2007.

Porterfield, Jason. *Shipwreck: True Stories of Survival.* Survivor Stories. New York: Rosen, 2006.

Vogel, Carole Garbuny. *Dangerous Crossings.* The Restless Sea. New York: Franklin Watts, 2003.

INTERNET SITES

FactHound offers a safe, fun way to find Internet sites related to this book. All of the sites on FactHound have been researched by our staff.

Here's how:

1. Visit *www.facthound.com*

2. Choose your grade level.

3. Type in this book ID **1429600896** for age-appropriate sites. You may also browse subjects by clicking on letters, or by clicking on pictures and words.

4. Click on the **Fetch It** button.

FactHound will fetch the best sites for you!

31

INDEX